# Make Money Online

# Without Spending Any Money

## By

## Ron Charleston

# Disclaimer

# Table of Contents

# ACKNOWLEDGMENTS

A big thank you to my publisher for helping me put this together.

# Introduction

In my book, *The Dream is Gone: Economic Survival in 21st Century America*, I wrote about the need to expand your sources of income, so you are not dependent upon any single source. I gave a few examples of this in chapter 8, with an emphasis on making money online. In this book, I have gone into more detail about making money online, but only those opportunities that will cost you nothing but your time. The reason for this is that there are simply too many ways to lose money when attempting to make money on the Internet. You need to walk before you run.

The Internet is filled with ads pitching some product that will allow you to make money at home from your computer. Some of these advertisements will go so far as to claim you can get rich, or at least make an outrageous sum of monthly or yearly income.

Some of this money can supposedly be made in a matter of days. How much of this is legitimate? Not much, and at the very least, the claims are exaggerated. Can you make money on the Internet? Yes, but unfortunately, it is not usually a path to riches. But you can make money, and this money can be important to survive in today's world. You may be looking for a full-time income or just some money to supplement your present income, but the good news is that it is possible to make money and with no investment other than your time. Some of these ideas in this book may not be right for you while others may be a good fit. Some of these methods produce more income than others. Some produce money quickly while others will take a more patient approach. I have tried to be as specific as possible to give you the best chance at making money online starting with nothing. Everything in this book is something that I have made money doing. Some areas, I have succeeded more than others, but this has a lot to do with my abilities and personality. What works best for one person, may not work as well for another.

# Section 1

# Mechanical Turk

I want to begin by talking about Mechanical Turk because I do reference it a couple of times in other sections of this book. Mechanical Turk is a website created by Amazon that is dubbed Artificial Artificial Intelligence. Its purpose is to take a large project and allow for its completion in a quicker time frame than it normally would be completed by a single person or a small group of people. This is accomplished by breaking it down into smaller tasks that a single person can complete quickly. When taken as a whole, a large group of people, working on these small tasks, can complete a large project quickly. This type of work is something that a computer program would be hard pressed to complete, or any some cases, it would be possible, but only with elaborate software. This, of course, makes the project too expensive. A large group of people engaging in micro tasks is often the most cost effective approach.

There are a variety of tasks that are posted on this site, some of them have certain qualifications; the most common is the percentage of hits (tasks) that you have had approved. Amazon acts as a broker between the worker and the requester. It is the requester that pays Amazon, the money you earn is specified in the hit your are doing. Once it is approved, the money is transferred to your Amazon Mechanical Turk account.

I first heard about Mechanical Turk over 10 years ago. I'm not sure where, but it may have been in the Amazon book seller's forum. When I first signed up for an account, there wasn't much  work listed because they were in the early days of beta testing. I remember the main job was one in which Amazon was the requester. There would be a series of photos of businesses that were taken from a moving vehicle with a camera mounted on top. The worker had to select the photos where you could read the business sign. In hindsight, it may have related to the early days of Google's street view that you see on their maps.

I remember the pay of each task was high for the time it took to do the work. But Amazon was willing to pay well because they wanted a lot of workers to debug their Mechanical Turk system. I worked seven days a week, and the money piled up. Eventually, this work died down, and it was replaced by requesters unrelated to Amazon. Naturally, the pay dropped, but there were new opportunities to be found. My first transcription work that I describe in Section 4 is one example. I also found my first content writing jobs here on Mechanical Turk. This led me to higher paying work outside of Amazon. I also made a lot of money taking surveys. Most of these surveys were conducted by college researchers.

I don't do much work there now, but occasionally, in the early morning, I will do a few surveys if the pay is good. The other day I was notified by email of a follow-up survey to one I had done six months ago. The original survey was 10 minutes of my time for $2.00. The follow-up was another 10 minutes, but it paid $10. I'll take that kind of money all day long. Unfortunately, that type of work isn't available all day long.

## Mechanical Turk and Amazon Payments

It's easy to get started at Amazon Mechanical Turk, simply go to their website and sign up for an account. However, there are a couple of things you should know to make your experience there easier. The first is that you will need an Amazon Payments account in order to get paid, although you can choose Amazon gift certificates in lieu of a cash payment, I prefer the money. You will need a bank account to transfer the money to, but you don't need a traditional bank account such as a checking account. A prepaid debit card will do just fine. A prepaid debit card is a bank account and will have a routing number as well as an account number. This is all you need to transfer money. When I first used Mechanical Turk, the minimum balance to transfers to your bank account was $10.00. It is now only $1.00.

## Turkopticon : An important tool to use with Mechanical Turk

Along with an Amazon Payments account, you should also have a Turkopticon account as well as their browser extension. Turkopticon is a website that has reviews of most of the requesters on Mechanical Turk. This can be a real time and money saver because reviews and ratings will keep you away from the bad requesters. Those who have have done at least one hit for the requester can leave a review and rating for them.

There are four categories: communicative, generosity, fairness and promptness. Communication refers to how well the requester responds to questions, promptness refers to how quickly they pay, fairness relates to their acceptance or rejection of your work, and generosity relates to how well they pay for the work. All four criteria are rated on a scale of 1 to 5. Reviewers are also allowed to flag a requester, if they believe the hit violates Mechanical Turk's terms of service. Common examples of this include various requests for a worker's personal information.

Although you can go directly to the website and look up each requester, there is a browser  extension that displays all of these ratings inside of  Amazon Turk as you look through the available tasks. There is an extension available for both Firefox and Chrome.

You can create a Turkopticon account and download the extension at their website:

https://turkopticon.ucsd.edu/

This browser extension is free to use.


The Mechanical Turk website can be found at:


https://www.mturk.com/mturk/welcome

# Section 2

# Content writing

Every website or blog you visit on the Internet is filled with articles and other information. What you may not know is that much of this written content is purchased. There are several ways this is done, but one popular way is to buy it from a company that specializes in producing it. A business or website owner specifies what they need, and then a content company has their writers produce the required content. If you enjoy writing, this may be something to try. And it doesn't cost anything to start doing this type of work.

Although the pay varies, it is generally low by professional writing standards, and because this type of writing places an emphasis on speed. So if you want to make a living wage, you must learn to write fast. This is not easy to do, and for many people, it is not even possible. But if you don't have any experience writing and are thinking about writing as a career, this is a great place to start. At the very least, it can be a part-time job, and you don't ever have to leave your home.

A word of caution: Not all content sites are equal. Some of them are not very professional, and their pay rates usually reflect this. Getting payment for your work can also be an issue. But among those companies that are dependable, you can make a few dollars writing. The money is not great, but the practice you get by writing several days a week can lead to private clients and a career as a freelance writer. If you are interested, the following are a few sites that I have found to be good.

Textbroker

Writers Domain

Crowd Content

Content Runner

BlogMutt

Here are a few more with good reputations

Constant Content

The Content Authority

Writer Access

Need an Article

Some of these content sites may already have enough writers, and you must wait for them to take on new workers. The best ones are usually the hardest to join up with. Some of them even have grammar tests. But you can still get your feet wet with other content writing sites that have lower paying rates. Just remember not to commit too much time into a particular company until you get a feel for what type of business you are dealing with. You also want to work with a company that has been in business for several years. Over time, these types of online companies have come and gone, and you don't want to get burned by one if they go out of business and still owe you money.

**Advice for content writing sites in general**

Read all of the rules and guidelines for submissions. Go slow at first, so you make as few beginner mistakes as possible, but understand that you will make mistakes. It takes time to get a feel for any content writing site. Most sites will allow clients to request revisions, and you will get them. Revisions are a part of freelance writing, no matter who you are working for or your skill level. Also, you need to learn to develop a thick skin for rejections. If there is a lesson to be learned, then remember the lesson and move on. But often there is no lesson. In this case, do not dwell on the matter. Place your article in a folder and use it for another client or another site at a later time. When an article is rejected, the work still belongs to you.

I have found that switching from one site to another can reduce my output. By writing on one site, I can maximize the number of articles I write. For this reason, the sites that pay the most are not necessarily the ones I make the most money writing at. Writers Domain, for example, is a good paying site; however they usually don't have a lot of work. You could spend most of the day just waiting for a job to show up.

Often the best strategy is simply to find a site that you feel comfortable with and focus your efforts there. I have found that some sites, even when there is work and the pay is good, it will take me longer to get an article done because I struggle to comply with the format required by the website or client. In other situations, I may spend too much time looking for the right job. So you need to factor in the total amount of time you spend to produce an article and not just the time spent writing it.

# Tools for writing

There are many things that will help you in your writing. Most of it can be found online, but some of it is available offline as well. The following is a short list of things that will help you improve your writing as well as your productivity. Some of these will cost money, and this book is about making money without any cash out of your pocket. But everything included here that costs money is optional. It may make writing easier. Also, the cost of acquiring or using any of these things is minimal.

## A word processor program

You need a program to use for writing, so you will need a good word processing program. I do not advise using the online word processors provided by content websites because it is easy to lose your work, if the website has any problems. It is best to do your work on your own computer, and then copy and paste it into the form. This way you will have a saved copy on your computer. If you already have a good word processing program such as Word, then you are done. But if you don't, you will need to get something. Notepad will not get the job done. You need something with a spell check and other functions. I recommend OpenOffice. It is open source software with a good word processing program aptly named OpenOffice Writer. It is free to use; the download page can be found here: https://www.openoffice.org/download/

This program is for windows based computers. If you have a Mac, you're on your own. I haven't used an Apple product since the Apple II back in 1982. However, I believe **TextEdit** on the Mac is the equivalent of Notepad on the PC, and I doubt this will be powerful enough to get the job done. You will need something better than this.

**Associated Press Manual Style Book**

This along with the Chicago Manual are the top two most important references to be found for writers. Because I cut my teeth at Textbroker, I use the AP manual, it was this reference that

I began my writing. I don't adhere to it exactly anymore, but it is still my main reference for consistency in my writing. You don't need one to begin writing online, and you can still get by with Google searches of AP standards, but they are still nice to have. The latest editions are expensive, but the truth is, you don't need the latest edition. You can find older editions at thrift stores or simply go to Amazon and shop for a used copy that is not current. In my opinion, an edition that is only four or five years old is fine. Our language doesn't grow or change that quickly.

**A grammar program**

There are a few outstanding software programs that will check your grammar as well as your spelling. These, however, cost money. When you're first starting out, I recommend a website called PaperRater. You can check your articles before submitting them to a client. The number of words in the document is limited to a few hundred, but this is usually less than a typical article you will be writing. In time, if you find you enjoy writing, you can upgrade to better software.

PaperRater can be found at

http://www.paperrater.com/

## Grammar and punctuation aids/tutorials

There are many websites that are dedicated to the English language that you will find helpful as a writer. I'm sure you will have yours as well. The following are a few of my favorites.

The Online Writing Lab

https://owl.english.purdue.edu/owl/

Grammar Bytes!

http://www.chompchomp.com/

Writing Explained

http://writingexplained.org/

In general, if you have a simple question about the definition of a word, the quick thing to do is type in define followed by the word. Google will bring up a link to the most popular online dictionaries.

The one I use the most is at https://www.merriam-webster.com/. Google will usually pull up the definition for you, but they are often displaying the results from a website, and the complete entry is not always listed in the Google search results.

Google is also good for quick grammar checks. Perhaps you need clarification regarding effect versus affect. Simply type in these two words, and there will be plenty of places to get the information you are looking for. Always pay attention to the website you are getting this information from because there is a lot of garbage on the Internet.

## A final word on content websites

Content mills have a bad reputation with those who consider themselves professional writers, but much of this opinion emanates from those with a superior attitude. Even the name content mill is pejorative, and I resist using it, preferring the term content website. Although most of these smug people make a lot of money writing, at least compared to those at content sites, the truth is that a writer must start somewhere, and many of these companies are a good place to begin. So called professional writers act like they just started writing for good pay from day one of their careers. Of course, this is not how life works. Not only is there a tendency to make more money at a profession over time, there is also the time it takes to learn and develop better skills. Professional writers who look down on those who write for content mills have amnesia. They have long since forgotten their meager beginnings.

Content websites are a great place to learn about writing, and you get paid for the work you do. Getting paid as you learn is a great thing, and anyone who gets paid for their work is a professional, no matter your level of skill. In addition, not all content mills are the same. The better ones, naturally, pay more money. And the truth is, a few of these sites are not necessarily a stepping stone, but are an end itself. An individual's goals for writing are not the same as everyone else. Perhaps you are looking for part-time work, or perhaps you are looking for flexibility in your working hours and want to work out of your home. These content websites offer a great range of possibilities.

And the pay is not as bad as many of these presumptuous professional writers would have you believe. It is true, that when I first started writing, I was cranking out 100 to 150 word articles for $0.66 a word. Yes, you read that right. I was working for less than a penny a word. But I kept at it and begin finding better paying work. At first, this was mostly   through content websites. My experience has been that you can make as much as $15.00 an hour on a good content site, but there are people who have made more. There are a couple of places I think I could make $25.00 an hour, but there simply isn't enough steady work, or the work available is on topics that are difficult for me to write about.

Ron Charleston

# Section 3

# Self-publishing

# eBooks

## Kindle

Another way to make money writing is to self-publish. In fact, self-publishing can be as easy as taking a document and turning it into a pdf file. But, of course, there is the problem of selling it. The most popular venue for purchasing eBooks is Amazon. Through their electronic reader, known as Kindle, they dominate the eBook market, controlling as much as 80% of all sales. They allow authors to self-publish by uploading their books to the Kindle library. Referred to as Kindle Direct Publishing or KDP, it is fairly easy to do, and it doesn't cost you a dime. Everything you need to know can be found on the Kindle website. They also have a community forum that contains a lot of good information as well as many nice, helpful people.

https://kdp.amazon.com/en_US/

I do have a few quick pointers to help you if you decide to go down this road. If you have your book saved as a word doc file, you're almost finished. You only need to make the width of your book 6.5 inches, but I'm not sure this matters because the device reading the file will determine the width. The height does not matter because your book, when read by a Kindle device, will be one continuous document. I keep my file at 11 inches, but this is only because I type in 8.5" x 11" pages. The left and right margins are not that important, but keep them at 0.9". The font is controlled by the Kindle user, but since I like to use 12 point Times New Roman, that is what my file is formatted in.

Images can be inserted into your document. I recommend .jpg file types and format them at 1000 pixels wide. If you are using windows, you can use the Paint program to resize your file, and save it. If you are using a Mac, you're on your own.

## Making a cover

There are many options to create a cover, but this book is about making money without spending money, so I will limit cover creation to those options that are free. Your first option is to use the cover creator program that is a part of Kindle publishing. It is easy to use, but whatever the finished cover is, you will only be able to use it on Kindle. There are other places to sell your eBook, and you will need a cover for those sites as well. But if you are only going to publish an eBook on Kindle, this may be a good option. If later you have a better cover, you can always come back and change the Kindle book cover.

Another free option online is cover making software. One that I have used in the past has been MyCoverMaker.com. You can sign up quickly for a free account and make a cover with point and click of your mouse. They offer more options if you upgrade to their pay version.

https://www.myecovermaker.com/

The good thing about making a cover here is that you can use it on Kindle as well as other eBook sites and even for a paperback on CreateSpace. I will discuss this later.

**Kindle Select – to join or not to join?**

Once you have your book published on Kindle, you have the option of joining Kindle Select. This program lasts for 90 days, and during that time, you cannot list your eBook anywhere else. In exchange for this exclusive listing, Amazon offers you two benefits. The first is promotional. During your 90 days enrollment, you can choose to have five days of a free eBook giveaway, or you can choose five days where you have discounted price sale. The second benefit is the Kindle Edition Normalized Pages program

(KENP). Kindle users who are enrolled in the Kindle Unlimited program or have a Prime membership can borrow books that are a part of the Kindle Select program. Amazon pays you, the author, a certain amount of money for each page that is read. This is typically less than a half of a cent per page read.

The free book promotion is often a good idea to get some visibility for your book. This can lead to a few book sales after the promotion ends. The money you earn from borrows will depend upon how long the book is and what genre it is written in. Non-fiction books don't often benefit as much as fiction books because they are designed to help people solve problems or to educate, and this is often a one time deal. Fiction, on the other hand is for entertainment. Sometimes portions of the book or the entire book is read again, at least more often than a non-fiction book. But even so, longer works of fiction will benefit more from the KENP program than shorter ones. Fiction books in popular genres of at lest 200 pages in length are the best candidates for success in KENP.

You can stick to amazon exclusively for your eBook, or you can attempt to branch out. Having your book enrolled in Kindle Select for the first 90 days is usually a good idea, but you should also attempt to sell elsewhere. You can always go back and sell exclusively on Amazon.

## Selling eBooks on other venues

If you are not enrolled in Kindle Select and you have a cover to use, such as one made at MyCoverMaker.com or perhaps one you have made yourself, there are many places you can list your book for free. You only pay a commission when a copy is sold.

There are many important sites that can provide a lot of sales, if your book is popular. Apple and Barnes & Noble are two of the biggest. The problem is that it takes time to format your book and upload to all of these sites. There are, however, two eBook services that you can use where you upload a single file, and then they will list it on various sites for you. You can call them eBook distributors, if you will. One is Smashwords and the other is Draft2Digital. Smashwords has been around for a long time, but I have never used them before. I do know they have requirements for formatting that you need to learn. With Draft2Digital, you can use the same file you used for your Kindle book. It is very easy. Draft2Digital is a younger company than Smashwords, but they have made a good reputation for themselves quickly. Part of this is because they do make it easy to use their service.

Both companies take a commission on top of the fee charged by the venue that is listing your book, but this is standard procedure for any type of distributor. They are acting as a middleman, so it will be more expensive. But I have found their service worth a slightly higher commission. It is a huge time saver to only upload a single file. In addition, in order to format for iTunes, the Apple platform, you need a Mac. Since I use a PC, I would need someone to do this for me, and that would cost money. But Draft2Digital takes care of the formatting for you. Just remember not to have any links to Amazon in your eBook or iTunes will reject your book. If that happens, all you need to do is remove the link. Apparently, Apple and Amazon don't get along.

# Print on Demand

Print on demand is exactly the what it sounds like. There is no inventory held anywhere. When an order is taken, a book is printed up and bound, then shipped to the customer. This concept has been around for many years and has even been in practice for a couple of decades, but it is only recently that machines specifically design for this type of product have been made, and the prices for them have come down.

Having said all that, print on demand services can be expensive, with one exception. Amazon has a service called CreateSpace. It is free to join, and you can upload your book along with a cover. After the book is approved, you are ready to make some money.

You will need to format your book, but this isn't difficult. You can do it yourself. If you write in Word or an equivalent program, then you can use one of the templates that CreateSpace provides, and simply cut and paste your document into the template. If you have a cover that you created outside of the Kindle cover maker software, you can use it for your book. You will want to use the same cover for all of your book formats. You also want the title of your book to be exactly the same as your Kindle, so the Amazon software will recognize this and connect both books together in the Amazon catalog.

You can order a proof copy, so you can hold it in your hands and leaf through it to see if you want to publish it. But this costs money. Granted, it is about $6.00, but this book is about not spending any money. Without any cash outlay, I recommend looking carefully at the book online with their proofing software. The book appears on your screen exactly as it will appear in print, and you can turn the pages one by one. If you like what you see, then you approve the book for publishing and it will appear in the Amazon catalog. It may take a couple or three days to be searchable, but once it is indexed by Amazon the search engine, you will be able to go the Amazon and search for your book just like you have done for other books and authors in the past.

Keep in mind that whether you are enrolled in Kindle Select or not, you are free to have a paperback through CreateSpace. It is a separate part of Amazon.

Ron Charleston

# Section  4

# Audio Transcription

**Audio Transcription**

This is a needed service and is something you can do from your home. Basically, you receive an audio file and transcribe what you hear into text. There are different sources of audio that people want this service for. Speeches, lectures and podcasts are only three examples. I did this work for a while. The entry level pay isn't very good, but if you stick with it, there is the possibility of making a living at it. Some of the high end work involves medical transcription work, but this takes specialized training. However, the required classes are not extensive, and if you find that you like audio transcription work, you can pursue it further. Medical transcription being only one possibility.

The best way to start is sign up with a company that acts as a broker. These companies essentially have the same business model as content writing companies. They solicit orders from clients that need transcription work, and then offer it to a group of subcontractors such as people like you. You are working for yourself, but will get paid by the transcription company when your work is approved. This is a good way to start in this field because you don't have to go looking for customers, and you can gain valuable experience. I worked for several different companies years ago when I started out. The first couple of companies I worked for I found on the Mechanical Turk site, but I later branched out to others on individual websites. Each company has its own guidelines and rules for transcription, so you will need to be well versed in their requirements for formatting.

One example of a company I did transcription work for was Speechink. Most of the work was transcribing interviews of people involved in car accidents for attorneys. For legal reasons, all words, even sounds, had to be transcribed. As I wrote this, I was curious to see if this company was still around. They are, but they are now called Speechpad Worker. I remember having to take a test; my score was high enough that I qualified to do work for them. I imagine most of these companies require you to take a test. The pay wasn't high, but it was a good entry point for audio transcription work. At times, the work was tedious, but what work isn't? Eventually, I gave up transcription work, but it was due to a hearing problem I developed.

If you find that you like this kind of work, you will want to invest in transcription software and a foot pedal. This latter piece of equipment is connected to your computer with a USB port. It allows you to start and stop an audio file, so you can keep both hands on your keyboard to transcribe. It is well worth the money to buy one because your productivity will increase. But you can delay the purchase of one until you decide you want to pursue this line of work further.

As far as software, there are various programs for this type of work. Some are cheap; others are more expensive. These programs allow you to download a file, and then change the volume, bass, treble and can filter out some of the noise. The program I used years ago was Express Scribe, a Windows based software. It was a free download back then and still is today, although I'm sure it has gone through several versions since I used it. Back then, the free version did not have many of the options that the full version had, but the full version was available at a reasonable price. Of course, there are likely other software programs available as well. The point to remember is not to invest a lot of money in transcription work until you have a feel for whether you want to pursue it further.

# Section 5

# Paid Survey Sites

Corporations want to know your opinions about a host of things, and they are willing to pay you to get this information. The problem for many companies is finding out who and where these people are. This takes time and money. The solution to this problem has been solved by paid survey companies. These companies have people sign up for their survey site, and then have these same people provide profile information such as age, profession, gender, education, hobbies, income and other information that is important to a corporate marketing department.

The specific group of people that a corporation is interested in surveying is likely a subset of the data a paid survey site has on file. The corporation simply specifies which people they want to take the survey and at what rate of pay, then the paid survey site sends out invitations to take the survey by email. Those taking the survey will get paid by the survey site, who will hold back a small fee for their service. How much money you get paid will depend upon the amount of the survey. This is stipulated by the corporation that is paying for the survey.

You may be thinking, all of this sounds great. Where do I sign up? But before you get too excited, there are a few problems. First, you really need to belong to a group that marketing people want information about. The more in demand you are, the more surveys you will be asked to take. I can't tell you which people American businesses are most interested in, but I can tell you that I'm not one of them. I have made some money taking these types of surveys in the past, but not enough to keep me interested.

You might be able to make two, three, maybe even four hundred dollars a month doing surveys, but you will need to be signed up with as many as 20 paid survey sites. And of course, have a profile that is in demand.

## A word of advice for anyone attempting to make money on paid survey sites

Be careful which sites you sign up for. These survey sites can come and go faster than some of the content sites. Also, you don't want to give out a lot of personal information to a site unless it has been around for a long time and has a good reputation. And never give out your social security information or banking information. PayPal works fine for payment; social security information is only needed for a 1099 tax form when you make more than $600 with a single survey site. And if you are making that kind of money on a single site and the site paid you, then they are a legitimate business that has a legitimate need for your Social security number for taxes. You are also an impressive paid survey taker.

Another piece of advice is to get a separate email just for survey sites because you will be bombarded by emails. The more sites you sign up for, the more emails you will get. There are some sites that will email you more than others, but taken as a whole, you need to have a separate email. Trust me on this.

Also, never pay to join a site. Paid survey sites make their money from companies that pay them because of the quality of their consumer database. They should not be collecting any money from you, other than the fee deducted from your payment for their service.

I could list the paid survey sites that I have used and that also have good reputations, but the problem with this is that businesses on the Internet seem to always be going through changes. Instead, let me give you a good site that keeps track of paid survey sites and are rated by the people who use them. The site is called Survey Police. It is well named as it stands guard as a sort of consumer protection for those who use survey sites to make cash.

Here is their link.

https://www.surveypolice.com/

# Section 6

# Sell Your Services

There are several places on the Internet where you can sell your services, but Fiverr is the most popular for buyers, so that's where you want to be as a seller. I will limit my discussion to this website.

## Fiverr.com

This is a website where you can offer a variety of services, or gigs as they're called on Fiverr for $5. That may not sound like much, and in truth, it isn't, but many people have made good money by offering extras or add-ons to their services. At this website you offer a basic service for $5. This is all that a customer is required to purchase, but if the extras are attractive, the average order will be much higher.

It doesn't cost anything to sign up, nor does it cost anything to list your gigs and extras. Fiverr will take out 20 percent of the total order, including the basic $5. So if the only purchase is the basic $5 gig, you will be making $4. There is also a two percent charge for transferring money to PayPal, but this is what PayPal charges Fiverr, so they are passing on the cost to you. This means you are making $3.92 for a basic gig. But if you can do these jobs quickly and to a high standard, the money may still be worth it, even without any extras being purchased.

You can browse the Fiverr website to see if there are services that you may be able to provide given your skills. I have purchased many jobs at this site, and I have been a seller for a short period of time. The following are a few tips and observations.

When I was a seller, I tried selling articles. I kept the word limit to 400. One problem I encountered was the number of revision requests I experienced. Believe me, I had nothing to do with most of this. Often a customer simply didn't know what they wanted before they placed their order. The lesson here is that regardless of what your service is, you need to limit the number of revisions to the job.

In general, you want to make sure you are clear about what the customer is getting for their $5. Once this is clear, you can explain the extras that you offer. You should take time to research your competition, so you are not pricing yourself out of the market. In the case of the basic service for $5, you need to offer a comparable amount of work for the customer's money.

Turn the work around in the time frame you claim to offer the service in. You can always offer an expedited extra charge for the order, but never be late. This will hurt your rating. The better your rating is, the more customers you will get. Although that is obvious to any platform, I have noticed that the better rated gigs show up higher in the Fiverr search results. Also, the quantity of gigs completed plays a large role in search result placement.

From a buyer's point of view, I can tell you that I have done a lot of repeat purchases. Once I have found someone a seller I liked, I go back again the next time I need the service. Of course, repeat business is at the heart of any successful business, so keep that in mind if you decide to take a shot at making money on Fiverr.

Visit the Fiverr website and explore the possibilities.

https://www.fiverr.com/

# Section  7

# Selling Your Unwanted Stuff

This section is only about selling your unwanted items online without any initial investment. It doesn't address buying inventory, because that costs money, and this book is about making money without any initial investment. Neither does it include selling on eBay. This popular site is not only expensive to sell anything, but if you list an item and it doesn't sell, it will cost you money.

Listing fees are expensive and it has been many years since I attempted to sell anything on eBay. I remember being frustrated as the fees kept going up and up. There are alternatives, namely a fixed listing site. This type of site allows you to list an item, and when it sells, they take a fee, usually a percentage of the amount sold. There are many websites like this on the Internet, and over the years, I have seen them come and go. However, Bonanza is a site that has been around for many years and continues to grow, and is the one that I recommend most. They get the most traffic, and will also send your inventory to Google's shopping search.

## Bonanza – how it works

Basically, they give you a free store, and you can list your items for free. They do have upgrade packages that provide you with more features, but again, this book is about making money without spending any money.

When it comes to selling something of value on Bonanza, there are two things that stand out. One is that they send their listings feed to Google. This is important because collectors are savvy. Certainly they will check eBay for the latest listings of what they collect, but they will also use Google. A quick search and a click on the shopping tab, and they can see listings all over the Internet. If you have something people are looking for, they will likely find it through Google, if you list it on Bonanza. You do have to opt-in for the feed to Google, because Bonanza takes an additional fee when you sell something that was found on Google through the Bonanza feed. The reason for this is the Google charges for accepting a data feed from an eCommerce website. But this fee Bonanza charges is small, and it only comes when a sale is made. My experience has been that it is worth it.

A second importation part about Bonanza is they have a make offer feature. You have to indicate that you will entertain the idea of a lower price when you create your listing. But if you are not sure how much you can get for an item, you can always go in high, and take a lower offer. For that matter, you can always lower the price later, but if you have something in demand, you may get an offer quickly when the price is a bit high. It's kind of exciting to get an offer for something you thought had little value. You list something for $100 and then a couple of weeks later, out of the blue, you are offered $70. Of course, you don't have to accept the offer, and you can make a counter offer, but the idea that suddenly someone is offering $70 for something you had sitting around your closet or the garage is amazing to me.

http://www.bonanza.com/

Ron Charleston

# Section 8

# Affiliate Marketing

Affiliate marketing has enormous possibilities for an income stream on the Internet. The biggest problem is that it costs money, at least for advertising. However, it is possible to get started, and even make money, doing this without spending a dime, so I have included it in this book.

If you are not familiar with affiliate marketing, it is simply selling a company's product as an independent sales representative in the manufacturing industry does. This type of selling has been around for decades, but in the Internet world, it takes the form of paying someone a commission for sending a customer to a website, and having that person make a purchase while they are there. Unlike the manufacturing model of sales representation where you signed up with a company and were given an exclusive territory, the Internet is one big territory for the affiliate salesperson. Everyone competes with everyone else who is an affiliate for the same company.

The basic way it works is you find a company with an affiliate marketing program, and fill out an application. Each company will have its own set of policies, so make sure you understand them before applying. Some companies are selective as to who they want representing them. Once you are approved, you will be given a code to include in a link to the product you are selling. Every time someone clicks on this link and they buy the product on the website of the company in your link, you will earn a commission or in some cases a flat fee.

The potential to make money with this type of selling is difficult to calculate. On the one hand, you are likely limited in how much you can make from a single product, but there are many companies that offer several products to sell. And you are not limited to how many companies you can sell for.

The biggest problem with affiliate marketing is getting people to find your link and click on it. Whatever links you have will likely be on a website or blog, so you will need to create one, and then drive traffic to your site. The best way to drive traffic to a site is through advertising. There are many ways to do this, but most of them cost money. In the long run, quality content on your website will bring in traffic. The type of content that marks you as an expert in a particular field. People will bookmark your site, and in time, you will place high in search engine results. For example, if you are a leading expert in professional photography and your site contains valuable information along with links to popular selling cameras on a website such as Amazon, there is a good chance you can make money with these camera links.

Speaking of Amazon, they are clearly the number one affiliate program in existence. They pay commissions on a wide variety of items on their site. It is easy to sign up for the program, and they provide a lot of support to their affiliate associates. A variety of tools are available, including link generators and sales reports. Everybody and his brother involved in affiliate marketing seems to have at least a foot in the Amazon pool, but they are the best. More information about their program can be found here:

https://affiliate-program.amazon.com/

Although large companies have their own affiliate programs, smaller companies, entrepreneur with startup companies do not. If they want to promote their product using affiliate marketing, they must do it through a broker. Without question, the largest online company with this type of broker business model for affiliate marketing is ClickBank. They have been around for many years, and they take the risk out of dealing with these smaller companies. Naturally, they take a percentage as a middleman, but you always get paid. There are many people who have done well with some of the products listed on the ClickBank site. They literally have millions of products to choose from. Their site can be found at:

http://www.clickbank.com/

**A free blog for affiliate marketing**

Although it is difficult to succeed in affiliate marketing without spending money, it is not impossible, especially if you have specialized knowledge and can build a website or blog using only your time. In order to do this with no initial investment, you will need a free blog. I would recommend Google's blogger. It doesn't cost you anything, and you can create a few affiliate links. You still need to get traffic to your site. However, if you want to play around with affiliate marketing without spending any money, this is the way to do it.

You can explore a free blog from Google at their free blog site.

https://www.blogger.com

## Google AdSense

Google offers a way to automatically monetize your blog by enabling AdSense. This is a program in which Google will display advertisements of their choosing, and if someone clicks on the ad, you will earn a small amount of money. But this money is literally pennies, and it doesn't compare to affiliate marketing. In addition, you can't control what is being advertised on your blog or website, and I don't like that. Although you can enable AdSense with any website or blog, it is as easy as a single click with Blogger. So I feel obligated to mention it, but don't expect much potential income from this, even if you have a lot of traffic. I gave up on AdSense revenue years ago. Affiliate marketing is a different story.

## WordPress.org and WordPress.com

### WordPress.org

While I'm on the topic of blogging, I need to mention WordPress. It is the most popular blogging software on the Internet. You may also have heard that it is free. However, there are two ways to get a free WordPress blog. The first is to go to WordPress.org and download the program for free and install it on your computer. You can then create your own blog with WordPress. But you will still need a domain name and a web hosting service to host your blog. Although this is not expensive, it does cost money. If you decide to get serious about affiliate marketing. I highly recommend this path.

### WordPress.com

WordPress.com is similar to Goggle's Blogger. You get a free blog and you get a domain name that is hosted by Wordpress. There is nothing to buy. There is one big difference. You cannot use affiliate links, at least not if the blog is for the main purpose of producing income. They do allow an affiliate link here and there on a blog designed for a social purpose. Therefore, this version of

WordPress is not something of value for affiliate marketing.

Ron Charleston

# Conclusion

With the exception of Mechanical Turk and paid survey sites, all of the things written about in this book I have made money doing at some time in the past, or I am still doing today, either part time or full time. Although I devoted all of my waking hours to Mechanical Turk during the beta testing phase, and I made plenty of money, that was only for a few weeks. Paid survey sites I never made a lot of money doing. Some people claim to have made a few hundred dollars a month doing surveys. I don't think I ever heard a story of more than $400 a month, at least a story I believed. However, there does seem to be the potential to make a part-time income for people that companies are interested in.

Everything else has the potential to be a part-time or full-time income, and some of these can lead to careers. Of course, with selling your unwanted stuff in Section 7, eventually, you will run out of things to sell. But the experience may help you develop the skill to acquire more inventory, used or new. The Internet is flush with people making their living selling products. Affiliate marketing is not likely to earn you much money as outlined in this book, but you can get your feet wet without spending any cash. You may discover you have a flair for it.

Content writing can be a second income, but it can also lead to a career in freelance writing. Audio transcription is another profession people make a living at. The services you offer on a site like Fiverr can lead to self-employment from your own website, or perhaps locally, offline. As for self-publishing, a bestseller could lead to a contract with a major publisher who wants to buy the book rights, or maybe you could become the next Simon and Schuster.

**A final word of advice**

Spend no money or as little money as possible when attempting to make money in any area of the Internet, at least in the beginning. There are too many scams on the web, and they are always promising great wealth, at least if you give them your credit card number. Learn as much as you can, but avoid expensive courses. Even the ones that have good information are usually outrageously overpriced. There is a lot of money to be made online, but it doesn't come easy, nothing ever does.

Ron Charleston

# About The Author

For more than 20 years, Ron Charleston worked in the field of electrical engineering, but after a sudden layoff, he found himself unemployed and with few career options in sight. This led to a new outlook on his personal finances and income generation. Today, Ron is self-employed, and makes his income exclusively from online activity.

Ron Charleston

# Other publications from Teela Books

## Sports and Horse Racing Betting Systems That Work! by Ken Osterman

The book contains some of the best sports betting systems from Ken Osterman. These are systems that he has used himself successfully at both racetracks and sports books. The rules for each system are clearly explained and the systems are explained clearly so it is understood why they work. Tips for improving these systems are also provided.

There are 10 systems in this book that cover horse racing, football and baseball. Here is a list of the systems with the sport that is covered and the title of the system.

Horse racing

Quarter Horse - The Hidden Speed Horse Angle

Thoroughbred - Best Jockey – Long shot Method

Thoroughbred - Bet the Fastest Horse

Thoroughbred - Show a profit down under

Harness - The qualifier advantage

Harness - Morning Line Overlay

Sports Betting

NFL Football - The Injured Star

NFL Football - The Hat Trick

Baseball - The AAA Surprise

Baseball - The Underdog Advantage

This book is currently available:

In Kindle format on Amazon:

http://www.amazon.com/dp/B00JTMWDNM

It is also available on iBooks, Barnes & Noble, Kobo, Inktera, Scribd, 24Symbols, and Tolino.

It is also available in Paperback on Amazon

http://www.amazon.com/dp1507800142

# The Path to Harness Racing
# Handicapping Profits by Douglas Masters

The Secrets of Harness Race Profits Revealed!

This book represents three decades of handicapping and betting harness races and is a summary of observations that are important to being a winning player. This book summarizes the conclusions on what made the author a winning player. There is no magic formula to become a winning player and the author is the first to say that there is more than one road to profits. This book is the road taken by Doug Masters to becoming a winning player. Becoming a winning player is part art and part skill, so it is impossible to summarize it as a mechanical method; however, Doug attempts to outline his process in the second half of the book.

This book may be difficult for beginning harness handicappers to read because it does not explain any basic terminology. There are, however, glossaries of harness racing terms online as well in the racing programs of harness tracks.

There are no winning examples in this book.

This is a quote from the author in the introduction.

"You will find no past performances listed in this book; this is intentional. Anyone who has been around harness racing for even a few years has probably read various books and publications offering a handicapping system. All of them will have examples of how a handicapping system or angle picked a winner. Anyone can do this, especially when so many of these authors are working backwards from the winner. To me, it is simply a waste of time. And besides, only a mediocre or inexperienced handicapper is going to believe there is a single path to success in wagering. This book consists of my observations of the sport and how it relates to my own handicapping perspective. If you are looking for a system that represents some sort of absolute truth, you're looking in the wrong place."

Topics include: Handicapping Factors, Drivers, Horse Form, Speed, Pace, Class, Post position, Track, Statistics, Betting multiple racetracks.

This book is currently available:

In Kindle format on Amazon:

http://www.amazon.com/dp/B00I5B13MU

It is also available on iBooks, Barnes & Noble, Kobo, Inktera, Scribd, 24Symbols, and Tolino.

It is also available in Paperback on Amazon

http://www.amazon.com/dp/1508707553

# Type 2 Diabetes: From diagnosis to a new way of life

# by Matthew Lashley

From the author

This book tells the story of how my diabetic condition was discovered, my denial of the condition, then the work done to get my glucose level to levels that are close to normal. There is no magic solution to treating type 2 diabetes, but I hope the information that I gathered and applied to my own life may be helpful to everyone struggling with type 2 diabetes. There is no cure, and I will have this condition the rest of my life. However, type 2 diabetes can be treated and controlled with the proper approach and lifestyle changes. You can have a better quality of life with a diet that is compatible with this disease.

Topics include:

From denial to self-blame

How I found out what type 2 diabetes was

Acceptance and getting down to work

Medication

Type 2 diabetes is a serious illness

How many carbohydrates per day should the limit be?

My target glucose levels

Foods to eat and foods to avoid

The importance of fiber in the diet

Eating out at restaurants

Is the damage from type 2 diabetes reversible?

Can type 2 diabetes be prevented?

This book is currently available:

In Kindle format on Amazon:

http://www.amazon.com/dp/B00IRJ9L1K

It is also available on iBooks, Barnes & Noble, Kobo,

Inktera, Scribd, 24Symbols, and Tolino.

It is also available in Paperback on Amazon

http://www.amazon.com/dp/1508826005

# The Quick and Dirty NFL Football Handicapping Method By Ken Osterman

The purpose of this book is to explain a fundamental approach to making a profit betting on professional football games, especially for those with little time to handicap them.

This method will help you find an overlay in the point spread using the simplest and quickest method possible.

The Quick and Dirty NFL Football Handicapping Method teaches you how to create your own point spread for each game in the NFL.

# Table of Contents

Improving this method


Mistakes to Avoid


Conclusion



This book is currently available:


In Kindle format on Amazon:

http://www.amazon.com/dp/B00NX9X81I



It is also available on iBooks, Barnes & Noble, Kobo, Inktera, Scribd, 24Symbols, and Tolino.


It is also available in Paperback on Amazon

http://www.amazon.com/dp/151202614X

# Betting on Major League Baseball

# The Underdog Method By Ken Osterman

The essence of any good baseball handicapping system is to find games to bet on that will result in long-term profits. In other words, finding overlays. The Underdog Method uses an approach to not only find these good bets, but does so by creating a money line that can be compared to the one offered by sports books.

Author and sports gambler, Ken Osterman, explains this system in an easy-to-understand way, and then uses an entire day of baseball games as examples. Each game is handicapped per the rules of the Underdog Method, and then a betting line is created. This line is compared to a specific sports book's money line. It is then decided, based upon specific rules, whether a good bet exists or not.

Although demonstrating the effectiveness of any betting system is limited in a book, the approach to Major League Baseball betting using the Underdog System is significantly different than the simple angles and methods seen elsewhere.

This book is currently available:

In Kindle format on Amazon:

http://www.amazon.com/dp/B01220NL8I

It is also available on iBooks, Barnes & Noble, Kobo, Inktera, Scribd, 24Symbols, and Tolino.

It is also available in Paperback on Amazon

http://www.amazon.com/dp/1515180646

# Free Things To Do on the Las Vegas Strip A Self-Guided Tour By Matt Lashley

The Strip is world famous and not only for the casinos, but also for the many things to see and do. Of course, a lot of what you can do here costs money, but there are a number of things to do that are free.

This book is a self-guided tour, taking you step by step down the Strip to visit all of the notable free things to do. This excludes most of the photo opportunities, because the entire length of the strip is filled with places to take a photo of you, your friends and relatives. Only a few places of interest, directly in our travel path, are mentioned. Also, shopping sites have been excluded except for three unique stores of interest on the Strip.

The trip begins at the Welcome to Fabulous Las Vegas sign and ends in the downtown portion of Las Vegas Blvd. This is the old section of Las Vegas and is not considered a part of the Strip. I have included it to provide a complete Las Vegas experience.

This book is currently available:

In Kindle format on Amazon:

http://www.amazon.com/dp/B01EW6DWXY

It is also available on iBooks, Barnes & Noble, Kobo, Inktera, Scribd, 24Symbols, and Tolino.

It is also available in Paperback on Amazon

http://www.amazon.com/dp/1533524084

# Stealth Betting Systems for Winning at Casinos by Luke Meadows

Stop Losing and Start Winning in Las Vegas casinos!

Author and casino gambler, Luke Meadows, explains his betting methods he uses in Las Vegas casinos in an easy-to-understand way. There are casino systems for the games of roulette, craps, blackjack, Let It Ride, and Keno. Mr. Meadows is convinced that your best chance of winning is small wins using smart gambling systems, and to do this without bringing attention to yourself – a stealth mode of casino gambling.

In all of this time Luke, like most of us, has experienced both winning and losing. Over time, his trips to Las Vegas have produced more profits than losses. The reason for this is his method of gambling at casinos. A method that he has honed and fine-tuned to the point where he has the best chance of winning, while at the same time, keeping his losses low.

This book is currently available:

In Kindle format on Amazon:

http://www.amazon.com/dp/B01KGSN63S

It is also available on iBooks, Barnes & Noble, Kobo, Inktera, Scribd, 24Symbols, and Tolino.

It is also available in Paperback on Amazon

http://www.amazon.com/dp/1537175939

# The Dream is Gone Economic Survival in 21st Century America Say No to Credit – Say No to Banks by Ron Charleston

For many Americans, it may seem like they are moving rapidly out of the middle class and towards poverty. This is not just a feeling. The middle class is disappearing, and you need to take steps now to insure your economic survival, today and into the future.

Regardless of the propaganda on television about the American dream, the agenda for the average American is survival. This book teaches you how to get out of debt and stop using credit. Unlike what you hear from the mainstream media, good credit is not desirable. You want is to avoid using credit altogether. In these pages you will learn why and how to do it. You will also learn the danger of using banks, and how to get around having a traditional bank account.

Economic survival means breaking free from a system that takes from you and offers nothing in return. The only solution is to break free from it. Break free from credit and other economic traps laid by corporations that are only interested in profits. In these pages you will learn how to rid your life of debt and live free with cash based finances.

This book is currently available:

In Kindle format on Amazon:

http://www.amazon.com/dp/B01MY926X7

It is also available on iBooks, Barnes & Noble, Kobo, Inktera, Scribd, 24Symbols, and Tolino.

It is also available in Paperback on Amazon

http://www.amazon.com/dp/1542637066

# Things To Do in Las Vegas Off the Strip – Away from the Neon Lights by Matt Lashley

From the author:

This is a follow up to my book, *Free Things to Do on the Strip: a self-guided tour*. The following are things to do that are off the Strip, away from the neon lights – well, at least most of it. Some of these things are free, and I have grouped them in the first section. Everything else will cost you money. However, I have only included those things to do off of the Strip that are reasonable in price. Most of these places are not too far from the Strip and can be easily reached by car. I have also tried to list prices and hours of these places, but you should always check the websites or call for current information.

I have also included things for kids to do in Las Vegas. Kids can get bored quickly, and this city was not designed for them. There are a few arcades in some hotels, and there are pools for swimming when the weather is warm, but parents can run out of ideas to provide entertainment for their children quickly. Many of these destinations are suitable for families

This book is illustrated with photos.

This book is currently available:

In Kindle format on Amazon:

http://www.amazon.com/dp/B071XT3VYF

It is also available in Paperback on Amazon

http://www.amazon.com/dp/1545575398

For the latest information about our publications, along

with articles by some of our authors, please

visit our website and subscribe to our newsletter


http://www.teela-books.com